Gay Notions

Four Short Plays On The Gay Experience

Floyd Stephen Alexander

<u>Dedication</u>

To the people I know who live by the life lesson of love, understanding, and acceptance. In a tribe, you can survive.

<u>Notice of Confidential Material</u>

The contents of **<u>Gay Notions</u>** are protected by manuscript infringement protection and copyright laws and are deemed the confidential property of FLOYD STEPHEN ALEXANDER. Unauthorized copying, disclosure, or use of this manuscript without prior consent is strictly prohibited. All inquiries and correspondence should be directed to:

Floyd Stephen Alexander

Author/Owner of Gay Notions

Telephone: 702.533.1583

Email: floydplaywrite@aol.com

Characters/ Scenes

Characters

Buster

Sophie

Emberto

Wayne

Belle Starr

Cuntsuela

Butch Anders

Holler Cassidy

Paulette

Clemit

Scenes

Buster

Leaves

Locks/Lashes

Packsberry Cattle Ranch

<u>Buster</u>

Buston ("Buster"): 16-year-old, rotund, black boy

Sophia ("Sophie") is an 18-year-old willowy, black girl of muted beauty.

Scene: Petemoss, Mississippi, 1966. Saturday, mid-afternoon. Buster and Sophia leave Mrs. Aldecker's Dress Shop and walk through the town.

Sophie:

Had to come to old lady Aldercker for a dress to wear to next week's baptism. That white sundress of mine has gotten short and clingy on me, and I'm just about naked. I liked what she showed me. I'll use my babysittin' money to pay for it.

Buster:

You see the colors in it? How it showed in the light? That ain't regular, from the factory cloth she uses. That's imported material right from Paris, France. Mrs. Aldercker told me she goes there every year for fashion. She comes back here and sells to the big city department stores.

Sophie:

Get out! That ain't a store-bought dress I was in?

(Buster confirms.)

Why does she live here?! She can't make no big money sellin' to us.

Buster:

This her home. She fell into dress-making 'cause she likes it. I do, too. She teaching me. Got me to invest in a subscription to a fashion magazine. Get it every month.

Sophie:

She said she discounted it. Instead of $30.00, it's $20.00. Why?"

Buster: '

Cause of me.

Sophie:

How much she pay you?

Buster:

I get paid $10.00.

Sophie: $10.00!!!!!! What you do for $10.00? (Sly smile comes over her face) Oh, I know what that's for.

Buster:

What for?

Sophie:

Mrs. A. is payin' for what comin' soon. She's wait for the right moment.

Buster:

I don't like what you insinuating.

Sophie:

Good word you learned in class. What it means is she wants to be <u>impaled</u> by your staff. It's understandable you not sniffin' around us. She can do better for you than we can.

Buster:

Is that how you see me? Is that how you see any colored mixin' with white livin' here?

Sophie:

You ain't that dumb to know a colored man an' a white woman bein' that close, and she givin' you that kind of money ain't from the goodness of her heart. Like I say, she can do better for you than I can. That explains a lot.

Buster:

You don't know a thing.

Sophie:

Why haven't you tried to get some from me? Enough have tried. Three succeeded. Doin' time with Port Loin now.

Buster:

Let's stop right here. (Both stop walking) Now come here close to me.

(Sophie is hesitant, but Buster gestures his demand, and Sophie does so)

I don't feel that way 'bout you. Not about any girl, anyway. So you don't have to wait for somethin' to happen. Now, why Mrs. A. pay me $10.00 is because I earn it with my hands. That dress you had on, I made it. That kind of thing can't get out to nobody in town. If it do, nobody come to the shop to buy and Mrs. Aldecker lose her business. Now you understand.

Sophie:

I do. Let's keep walkin'. (They begin walking again) My uncle just like you. He in Richmond. Prettiest man you ever seen. When he come this way and stay with us, he and I go for ice cream. We sit out by the creek, and he tells me the place he goes to and the people he meets. He calls it his special place, and they are his special friends. Daddy fusses with him, and they get into a fight right in front of everybody. I ain't seen him for two years now.

Buster:

No special place or special people here in Petemoss. Just tippin' your hat or bendin' over to get along in the day and hide in your house at night. I don't think I can live here much longer. Told Grand Sal that. My Grandma Sally. She just waitn' for me to graduate Ashmore High, and I be movin' on. What I discovered out my magazines is that beauty, and fashion, and good manners can't be found in a place that doesn't know about either one. Your uncle, does he got someone special he keeps close to?

Sophie:

Yeah. Name's Esra. Been with him for eight years. Loves my uncle better than some of my cousins love their wives. Love ain't no story. It's for real.

Buster:

I love how a girl or woman looks when she sees how she can be in something that make her beautiful. That's a look I want see in the things that I make. And I don't give a good God'damn who can't understand why.

Sophie:

Thank you.

Buster:

What for?

Sophie:

Being a boy that wants to see me with clothes on than with them off. Especially when it make me look like I am just as beautiful as them women in the magazine, if that is who you are, you're the best man I know.

Buster:

I ain't your uncle, but I could go for an ice cream right about now.

Sophie:

I ain't your girl, but I'd have a better time eatin' it with you. You know, in all the time I known you, I call you Buster. Is that your real name?

Buster:

It's Buston. Buston Wood. I call you Sophie. That ain't yours.

Sophie:

Sophia. Mommy like the movie actress it come from. Means "wisdom".

Buster:

When it's just you and me, I'm a call you Sophia. It fits you.

(Sophie takes Buster's arm and wraps it around hers. She leans her head on his shoulder and they continue to walk. End of Scene.)

<u>Leaves</u>

Emberto: Rally captain representing the queer protesters

Wayne: Rally captain representing the straight protesters

Scene: City public park, early morning. Positioned on opposite sides of a barrier rope, Emberto and Wayne are making protest signs for a rally scheduled for today. Both are intense in their work while periodically eyeing each other.

Intro Music: Chopin's Nocturne No #2 in E-Flat Minor

Emberto:

I hope we can keep the rally peacefully today.

Wayne:

Your people stay on your side of the rope, we'll stay on ours. I don't want to be nowhere near you guys lisping and patting each other's ass.

Emberto:

Jealous?

Wayne:

Not on your life. What's your sign say? (Emberto picks up his sign and shows Wayne) **"<u>STOP THE FEAR. IT'S YOUR RIGHT TO BE QUEER!</u>"** Love it or leave it., that the idea.

Emberto:

It's not an alternative. What's yours say? (Wayne picks up his sign) **<u>"SCREW YOUR PRIDE, STAY ON YOUR SIDE!"</u>** Inclusive, yet divisive.

Wayne:

That melting pot idea don't hold water. We don't all mix well. You stand by those two broads that come on T.V. spouting that bull about "lifespan development"? It's natural to be like that?

Emberto:

Yes. Queerness is a normal development no different than being straight. What they're spouting, as you call it, is keeping kids from thinking they're nothing and blowing their brains out.

Wayne:

Their choice, their consequence. It's a fact that every time you people get an inch; you take a mile with some new letter movement. You started with "L", then came "G". Then "B". But that's not enough strange for you. Now it's "T",

"Q", "J" and "A". A great, big bowl of fruit loops. The damn cereal is now associated with you!

Emberto:

You're afraid.

Wayne:

I'm disgusted. It just looks like fear. I got a quote for you. Take it or leave it makes no difference to me. *"Do not be deceived: neither the sexually immoral, nor idolaters, nor adulterers, nor men who practice homosexuality, for neither will inherit the kingdom of God."*

Emberto:

Well, since we're bring God into it, I got one for you. *"I sing America in various carols. The mechanic who turns the wrench; the carpenter who measure the beam; the mason who readies the mortar; the boatman that sets the sail; the shoemaker that fashions my walk; the mother who grows what peoples the world; and we who are what is celebrated."* I paraphrased it from a poem by Walt Whitman.

Wayne:

You're countering what I said with a poem?!

Emberto:

I believe both have merit. It's about survival as well as celebration. You want us wiped off the face of the earth and claim it to be a mission from God.

Wayne:

Nobody's talkin' 'bout endin' you people! I, or should I say, folks who agree with me, don't like your ideas. What I think bothers you is you haven't met pushback like this before.

Emberto:

Who hasn't been met with ugly threats, beatings in the streets, cruel jokes, even ending one's life. Your banner said it clearly.

Wayne:

You're too sensitive.

Emberto:

You're too forthright.

Wayne:

I like John Wayne. That Whitman guy sounds like if he was ever put to the test to brave those words, he'd tumble like a stack of cards. American spirit is attitude, not aptitude.

Emberto:

You need a brain for civility. It's not all boast and brag. "Vive e lascia vivere."

Wayne:

Oh, what the hell is that?!

Emberto:

(Reassuring) Alright, I'll say it in English. It's "live and let live".

Wayne:

The first one of you throw a bra or a pair of underwear my way, the cops are going to get involved.

Emberto:

Just so you don't throw anything heavier. Like a brick or your fists. You and I have to keep our heads in this. Can we agree on that?

Wayne:

Sure. We're not shaking hands.

Emberto:

Your word is enough. (Looks off in the distance)
I can see everybody is starting to come.

(Wayne looks in the other direction)

Wayne:

Yep, here comes my group. Let's just keep it to
ourselves that we talked. Why mess up a good
rally?

Emberto:

My name's Emberto.

Wayne:

I knew it wasn't Ralph. Mine's Wayne. Can we
stop with the niceness?

Emberto:

Sure.

(Wayne and Emberto go back to their preparations as they
await their groups to arrive. End of Scene.)

<u>Locks/Lashes</u>

Belle Starr:

Caucasian Drag Queen

Cuntsuela:

Latino Drag Queen

Scene: Local dive bar. Two flamboyant drag queens, Belle Starr and Cuntsuela, take the stage at the Clip Box.

Belle Starr:

Hello, people! Glad to be out of the house?! Y'all needed to see a real woman.

Cuntsuela:

Thank you, darling, for pointing that obvious thing out.

Belle Starr:

I said a woman, not a child, honey.

Cuntsuela:

Ooh, don't be so mean.

Belle Starr:

When did this show become a duo? You just collect the money after I do my number.

Cuntsuela:

The real money comes after my performance.

Belle Starr:

The word "star" is in my name.

Cuntsuela:

The word "cunt" is in mine. Which name has more promise?

Belle Starr:

The ho' line is out back.

Cuntsuela:

Can we get on with the show?

Belle Starr:

Are you seeking a truce?

Cuntsuela:

I'm open to negotiations.

Belle Starr:

You know how we do it at the <u>Clip Box</u>. Jello-shots! Drink til' you have no reason to fight!

(A tray of cups is brought out and given to Belle Starr.) Alright, on my command, we drink. Waitress, give everyone a shot.

(Belle Starr waits until everyone is served.) Alright, bitches, hoist 'um high. One. Two. Three, gulp it!

(Everyone drinks.)

Cuntsuela:

That'll put hair on your junket. We got two more cups on the tray.

Belle Starr:

Them's for us. Take 'em. *(Cuntsuela takes the cups. She keeps one and gives the other to Belle Starr.)* Hoist 'um up high! One. Two. Three, gulp it! *(Both drink.)*

No man is an island who's got liquor. What was we takin' 'bout?

Cuntsuela:

Somethin' about ho'ing?

Belle Starr:

I know we was lifting something.

Cuntsuela:

Just our cups, baby. I want to sing.

Belle Starr:

We're going to, but I go first.

Cuntsuela:

Humming don't count. Ladies and gentlemen, Miss Belle Starr.

(Belle Starr lip-syncs <u>My Heart Belongs To Daddy</u> (Mary Martin Version) until completed.

Belle Starr:

Alright, Cunt-su-e-la, let me see your talent.

Cuntsuela:

Not if you want to go to jail.

Belle Starr:

Ladies and gentlemen, Senorita Cuntsuela. *(Cuntsuela lip-syncs <u>Dat's Love</u> from the film <u>Carman Jones</u> until completed.)*

Belle Starr:

I loved that movie. She was so beautiful.

Cuntsuela:

Yes, she was. They treated her like shit, you know.

Belle Starr:

Such ignorance. Beauty is a threat to those without it.

Cuntsuela:

I think my shot is wearing off. Who needs that. We goin' say goodnight to these wonderful people? Shit, why not!

Belle Starr:

Good-night, wonderful people! Stay well.

Cuntsuela:

Be safe.

Belle Starr/Cuntsuela:

And wash your dirty hands, so I don't catch a damn thing!

Belle Starr and Cuntsuela take their bows. End Of Scene.

<u>Packsberry Cattle Ranch</u>

Butch Anders: Head ranch hand

Holler Cassidy: Ranch owner

Paulette: New hire

Clemit: Assistant to Butch Anders

Scene: Outside the cattle corral, Noon. Holler Cassidy carries a hay bale to the corral. He throws it over into the corral and watches the cattle feed. Butch Anders rides in and gets off his horse.

Butch Anders:

We got the rocks moved from blocking the water. Didn't have to use dynamite. Just picks and shovels.

Holler Cassidy:

Good. Keepin' these cattle watered with this heat goin' up is what we needed. Now, get the boys to get the cabins ready for the greenhorns showing up tomorrow. Especially the single one we got to change from a tool shack. Move the tools and the like into the barn for now.

Butch Anders:

You know I ain't said too much about all this to you.

Holler Cassidy:

But you're gonna now.

Butch Anders:

This ain't a kid's camp for wannabes. Your idea to gettin' people in here to rope, herd an' brand real steers got me an' the boys confused.

Holler Cassidy:

I'm recruitin'. You know about that from playin' football at the high school. You boys got in 'cause y'all in the neighborhood. Local talent. I'm farmin' for new talent. Gettin' the government to help me do it, too. Minorities and women are my new draft picks. Cowboyin' going to be a lot different around here.

Butch Anders:

She goin' be thought different 'cause she's already gettin' special treatment with bein' separated from the rest of us. She's got her own bunkhouse.

Holler Cassidy:

I ain't goin' explain the reason why. Do I have to point out the difference between a bull and a cow? Please don't say I do.

Butch Anders:

How she look? Did she send a picture with her application?

Holler Cassidy:

I ain't running a beauty pageant. She lives and works on a farm; hates wearing dresses, and looking forward to learning the trade. Right now, she's lookin' better than some of you. She gets here tonight. You an' one other hand pick her up at the train station. You can't miss her. She'll be dressed in a t-shirt, jeans and boots. That's what I call ready to work.

(Cassidy leaves Anders. Anders pauses in thought, then speaks.)

Butch Anders:

If she's pretty, a steer won't be the only thing I brand.

Scene: Outside on the ranch, Morning. Anders and the new recruit, Paulette, walk together as he gives her an instructional tour.

Butch Anders:

I've shown you where the store house is; the galley where we eat, the branding circle, and the most important place, the privy. Just up a ways is the cattle corral. Good to let the steers look you over 'fore you start workin' them.

Paulette:

I want them to get to know me. Catch my scent. I get their trust, won't be bad when I go to brandin'.

Butch Anders:

Not so fast! You ain't touchin' one hair on their heads 'fore I think you ready. Greenhorns start at the beginning. Shovelin' shit and stacking hay. Hope you didn't bring anything nice to wear. Won't be worth a damn to nobody 'round here.

Paulette:

What I'm wearin' now is what I got for every day. Enough of you and the others lookin' at me like an x-ray.

Butch Anders:

X-ray??

Paulette:

Looking at me naked. Stare that hard, you want to see somethin'.

Butch Anders:

Nobody's interested in you! Don't start that bullshit harassment stuff! We don't take notice even if you are the first girl comin' to be a ranch hand.

Paulette:

Good. So call me by the name I told you and we'll keep things workable. Paul. My folks won't do it, but with this new company of friends, it fits right.

(Anders looks at Paulette)

Paulette:

You're staring again.

Butch Anders:

Tryin' to work it in my head. Callin' you "Paul" don't mean you goin' be doin' everything a Paul would do. You ain't bunkin' with the rest of us for a good reason.

Paulette:

That's something nature chose. Not me. I know you're good at passin' the word to the others. Do that.

(Anders gestures his acknowledgment)

Butch Anders:

Let's go see the beef.

(Anders and Paulette continue walking.)

Scene: Outside of cattle corral, Mid-afternoon. Paulette is sitting on the fence, watching cattle being let out of the corral. Another ranch hand, Clemit, is sitting with her.

Clemit:

Boy, look at them, run out the gate! This be the day. Brandin' day.

Paulette:

How come you ain't out there helping? You a steady here.

Clemit:

Can't move fast enough. Got a twisted leg.

Paulette:

Ride horseback. Put you at the head outside the gate so you can turn them towards the circle. Don't have to show off like Anders is doin' inside there.

Clemit:

Butch is a good hand. One of the best. Taught me since I come here. Use to poke me with a stick in my back to make me move faster with my stride. Worked too. I can catch up to a steer, rope it, and guide it back to the corral just as good as anybody with two good legs.

Paulette:

Like I said, you could ride. Go grab a horse and try it. I think Butch is havin' a little problem with the two caught up in the corner. I can't 'cause I'm green.

Clemit:

No, he wouldn't like that. I'd get in the way at the brandin'. Me running around with a hot iron.

(Paulette senses something in Clemit's comment. She pursues her thought.)

Paulette:

A hot iron pressed into bare flesh and seeing smoke rising like a cigarette stamped out in an ashtray. Smelling the meat burning and the steer cryin' out for mercy.

Clemit:

I don't like it, ok! I don't like doin' that job! Why you soundin' like that?! You a girl, ain't you?! Man, you a funny one, I tell you that!

Paulette:

Just one that got you thinking nights. Don't think I don't hear the peeking at my window to see. Did you get a good look to make sure? I'm the real deal, boy. Smooth legs, round butt, curved hips, pouched stomach topped off with nipple milk jugs. I got 'um, but I just don't know what all the fuss is about.

(Suddenly, Paulette and Clemit see a disturbance in the corral)

Paulette:

Oh shit, they got Anders pinned!

Clemit:

He can't get out of the way! Help!!! Help!!!

Paulette:

We're the help! I'm goin' in. Go get some hands to come up here.

(Clemit takes off. Paulette runs into the corral.)

Scene: Inside Cassidy's office, Next Day. Cassidy and Paulette are talking. The mood is solemn.

Holler Cassidy:

You said you wanted to know how Anders was when I got the news.

Paulette:

Yes.

Holler Cassidy:

You ain't family.

Paulette:

I jumped in and got him out. Just say I'm owed that much.

Holler Cassidy:

Broken arm, cracked ribs, and a black eye. If he'd been near the head, he'd have been gorged. You would have seen the worst of what happens around here. You got grit.

Paulette:

I don't run from trouble, if that's what you mean.

Holler Cassidy:

I mean, I'm a man down, and I need a hand.

Paulette:

I learn fast.

Holler Cassidy:

I don't. There's all men on this ranch. I like that. I can spit, cuss, and do a cartwheel with my pants around my knees if I want, and nobody gets their nose out of joint. If I take you on, I got complaints and a possible lawsuit for harassing your delicate nature. I don't need that.

Paulette:

Delicate nature don't apply to just women. You better take me on just to keep things equal.

Holler Cassidy:

I ain't callin' you "Paul". I'll give you respect for your talent, but you respect me for being from a different time. You're Paulette to me. That a problem?

Paulette:

Why they call you "Holler"?

Holler Cassidy:

I'm the strong an' silent type.

Paulette:

What's in a name?

(Cassidy gets Paulette's comment.)

Holler Cassidy:

Right. You know anything about filling out paperwork online? I got to do insurance on Anders.

Paulette:

I know my way around. Crank her up, and let's see what we got.

(Cassidy turns around in his chair to his computer. Paulette goes over and stands behind him. She leans in over Cassidy's shoulder and gives instructions. End of scene, end of play)

<u>About The Author</u>

Floyd was born in Philadelphia, Pennsylvania, during the golden age of Broadway classics (Long Day's Journey Into Night, Saint Joan, A Street Car Named Desire). A self-proclaimed "Philly Kid", Floyd got bit by the stage bug in high school and did high school and community theatre work to get some stage experience. Floyd is married to Nikki Alexander and has two daughters, Jessie and Blake Alexander.

Good-By High School, Hello College .... Attended Upsala College to study Theatre and Speech Communications (Workshop 90) and perfected his acting skills in various productions.

HB Studios, New York City .... After graduation, Floyd headed for the Village, signed up with HB Studios, and attended Cold Reading class. Got a few acting jobs but got homesick and headed back to Philadelphia.

Society Hill Playhouse .... Performed with the historic theatre company in some daring stage productions of Freedom of the City, Look Homeward Angel, and Fashions.

San Diego and Community Actors Theatre .... Floyd moved cross country to San Diego, California, entered military service, and decided to pick up the pen and write plays. It was at the Community Actors Theatre (CAT) that his first play, Dracula, was performed. What followed was Wolf Man, Here I Am! *Scribes (*written on military tour during the Gulf War), and James Baldwin: Portrait of a Writer.